Evaluation Guidelines for Representative Deliberative Processes

This document, as well as any data and map included herein, are without prejudice to the status of or sovereignty over any territory, to the delimitation of international frontiers and boundaries and to the name of any territory, city or area.

Please cite this publication as:
OECD (2021), *Evaluation Guidelines for Representative Deliberative Processes*, OECD Publishing, Paris, https://doi.org/10.1787/10ccbfcb-en.

ISBN 978-92-64-35418-0 (print)
ISBN 978-92-64-85901-2 (pdf)

Photo credits: Cover © João Marcelo Martins/Unsplash.com.

Corrigenda to publications may be found on line at: *www.oecd.org/about/publishing/corrigenda.htm*.
© OECD 2021

The use of this work, whether digital or print, is governed by the Terms and Conditions to be found at *http://www.oecd.org/termsandconditions*.

Foreword

To address citizens' calls for better representation and more opportunities to participate in decision making, public authorities from all levels of government are increasingly turning to citizens' assemblies, citizens' juries, and other representative deliberative processes to tackle complex policy problems. Starting in the 1980s, the trend has not only continued, but gained strength in recent years: the OECD has identified close to 600 examples, of which over 80 were implemented in the last two years alone (OECD Database of Representative Deliberative Processes and Institutions, 2021). This demonstrates the interest of OECD Members in representative deliberative processes to reinforce democracy.

Since its onset in 2019, the COVID-19 pandemic has brought unprecedented challenges for government and had direct implications for citizen participation, civic space, transparency, and access to information. The need for even more participation and deliberation to support democratic systems during an exceptional period has fuelled innovation in the field. For example, the impossibility of bringing people together physically has led practitioners to experiment with hybrid and online deliberation, demonstrating that such processes are possible, even under complex circumstances (Chwalisz, 2021).

Yet, the increasing use of representative deliberative processes exposes the lack of, and highlights the need for, specific guidance for their evaluation. In this context, the OECD has developed the guidelines in this report for policy makers and practitioners who want to evaluate the representative deliberative processes they initiate, commission, and implement. It establishes minimum standards and criteria for the evaluation of representative deliberative processes.

The purpose of this report is to encourage public authorities, organisers, and evaluators to conduct more comprehensive, objective, and comparable evaluations. This will allow policy makers, observers, and the public to gauge the quality of their representative deliberative processes, learn from past experiences, and, ultimately, help them initiate and develop better processes. In addition, a common framework for evaluations can generate data for comparative analysis.

These guidelines do not aim to be prescriptive or fully comprehensive. Instead, they provide a foundation of evaluation criteria on which more comprehensive evaluations can be built by adding additional criteria according to specific contexts and needs. The focus of this document is evaluation of the way deliberative processes are set up and conducted. Further research is needed, for instance, to provide guidelines for the evaluation of their long-term impact and wider effects.

These guidelines are part of the work undertaken by the OECD Public Governance Directorate on open government, and build on the 2020 OECD report *Innovative Citizen Participation and New Democratic Institutions: Catching the Deliberative Wave.* Furthermore, the OECD report *Improving Governance with Policy Evaluation: Lessons From Country Experiences* (2020b) demonstrates that policy evaluation practices can be a tool for governments to increase effectiveness and promote accountability and trust.

The methodology of developing these guidelines included: comparing existing evaluation frameworks for representative deliberative processes, iterative drafting with the OECD Advisory Group of Evaluating Deliberative Processes; collaborating with the Democracy R&D Network to develop the questions in the evaluation questionnaires; incorporating feedback from the OECD Innovative Citizen Participation

Network; and review and approval by the OECD Working Party on Open Government and Public Governance Committee.

The OECD's new Initiative on Reinforcing Democracy will provide further possibilities to explore how to strengthen existing democratic institutions and establish new ones though participation and representation. Building on this report, and the evaluations it inspires, lessons and recommendations could be drawn on how to design better deliberative processes, and practices can be analysed and shared to identify what works best in different contexts. Beyond evaluation, the OECD guide on *Eight Ways to Institutionalise Deliberative Democracy* (2021) identifies a range of ways to embed public deliberation and civic lotteries in existing democratic institutions. This work opens up new possibilities for governments to make meaningful citizen deliberation a permanent part of how public decisions are taken, as a key step towards strengthening democracy.

Acknowledgements

These guidelines were prepared by the OECD Public Governance Directorate (GOV) under the leadership of Elsa Pilichowski. They were developed under the strategic direction of Alessandro Bellantoni, Deputy Head of GOV's Open and Innovative Government Division and Head of the Open Government Unit. The guidelines were written by Ieva Cesnulaityte, a Policy Analyst in the Unit working on innovative citizen participation. They were developed in close collaboration with Claudia Chwalisz, Innovative Citizen Participation Lead, and the OECD Advisory Group on Evaluating Representative Deliberative Processes: Manuel Arriaga (New York University), He Baogang (Deakin University), Nicole Curato (University of Canberra), Rikki Dean (Goethe University Frankfurt), Yves Dejaeghere (Federation for Innovation in Democracy – Europe), Laurie Drake (Mass LBP), Stephen Elstub (Newcastle University), David Farrell (University College Dublin), John Gastil (Penn State University), Jane Mansbridge (Harvard University), Jane Suiter (Dublin City University's Institute for Future Media, Democracy, and Society), and Iain Walker (newDemocracy Foundation). A special thank you to John Gastil for comprehensive editorial and strategic advice, and to Danni Trainor (Think:Worthy Writing & Editing) for additional editorial assistance.

The guidelines benefitted from feedback provided by members of the OECD Innovative Citizen Participation Network and their colleagues: Sarah Allan, Graham Allen, Victoria Alsina, Lyn Carson, Obhi Chatterjee, Chris Ellis, Karin Fuller, Doreen Grove, Dimitri Lemaire, Josef Lentsch, Peter MacLeod, Benedikt Montag, Alex Renirie, Graham Smith, and Lazaro Tunon.

The guidelines also benefitted from strategic comments by OECD colleagues Monica Brezzi, Sara Fyson, Stephane Jacobzone, Mariana Prats, and Ivan Stola.

The OECD Secretariat wishes to express its gratitude to the Working Party on Open Government for reviewing the guide and to the Public Governance Committee who approved this report.

Table of contents

Foreword — 3

Acknowledgements — 5

Reader's guide — 8
    Key terms — 8
    How to use these guidelines — 9

Executive summary — 10

1 Conducting an evaluation: Why, who, and how? — 11
    1.1 Why evaluate? — 12
    1.2 Evaluating representative deliberative processes — 12
    1.3 Five principles of evaluation — 13
    1.4 Planning and designing for evaluation — 14
    1.5 Participatory evaluation — 15
    1.6 Peer evaluation — 15

2 What to evaluate? Framework, criteria, and measurement methods — 16
    2.1. Three-Step evaluation cycle — 17
    2.2 Framework — 18
    2.3 Evaluation criteria — 18
    2.4 Measuring the evaluation criteria — 22

3 Going beyond: Building on the minimum criteria — 25
    3.1 Wider impact and long-term effects — 26
    3.2 Evaluating institutionalised structures and processes for public deliberation — 28

Annex A. Further information resources … 30

Annex B. OECD Good practice principles for deliberative processes for public decision making … 31

Annex C. Member questionnaire … 33

Annex D. Organiser questionnaire … 40

Annex E. Questions for organiser reflection … 43

Annex F. Table of comparison of existing frameworks of evaluating representative deliberative processes … 44

References … 49

FIGURES

Figure 2.1. Three-step evaluation cycle of a representative deliberative process … 17

TABLES

Table 2.1. Framework for evaluating a representative deliberative process … 18
Table 2.2. Overview of the applicability of measurement methods for assessing evaluation criteria … 22

Table F.1. Comparison of evaluation criteria of existing frameworks of evaluation for deliberative processes … 44

Reader's guide

Key terms

- **Representative deliberative process:** A process in which a broadly representative body of people weighs evidence, deliberates to find common ground, and develops detailed recommendations on policy issues for public authorities. For shorthand, representative deliberative processes are often referred to as deliberative processes in this document. Common examples of one-off processes are Citizens' Assemblies, Juries, and Panels. There are also examples of institutionalised deliberative bodies, such as Agenda-setting Councils.
- **Members of a deliberative process:** The people selected via civic lottery to form a broadly representative group and take part in a representative deliberative process. Together, they form what is referred to as the **deliberative body**.
- **Deliberation:** Weighing evidence and considering a wide range of perspectives in pursuit of finding common ground. It is distinct from:
    - **Debate**, where the aim is to persuade others of one's own position and to 'win',
    - **Bargaining**, where people make concessions in exchange for something else,
    - **Dialogue**, which seeks mutual understanding rather than a decision,
    - and "**Opinion giving**," usually witnessed in online platforms or at town hall meetings, where individuals state their opinions in a context that does not first involve learning, or the necessity to listen to others.
- **"Rough consensus":** The aim is to find (as much as possible) a proposal or options that a large proportion of members can at least live with. When voting is used, it is either an intermediate step on the way to rough consensus, or a "fall back" mechanism when consensus cannot be reached.
- **Civic lottery:** A process used by public authorities to convene a broadly representative group of people to tackle a policy challenge. It is based on the ancient practice of **sortition**, which has a history ranging from Ancient Athens to the Doge of Venice. Today, it is used to select the members in Citizens' Assemblies and other deliberative processes. The principle behind a civic lottery is that everyone has a more or less equal chance of being selected by lot. There are two stages to a civic lottery. First, a very large number of people, chosen by lot, receives an invitation to be part of the process from the convening public authority. These randomly selected recipients can volunteer by opting in to the lottery. Then, amongst the volunteers, members are chosen by lot to be broadly representative of the public. **Civic lotteries aim to overcome the shortcomings and distortions of "open" and "closed" calls for participants**, which result in non-representative groups of people who do not mirror the wider population and attract those with the most interest or stake in the issue. (For greater detail, see Chapter 4 in OECD, 2020a.)
- **Evaluation of a representative deliberative process:** The structured and objective assessment of the design, implementation, and results of a one-off or institutionalised representative deliberative process. More specifically, in this document evaluation refers to *ex-post* evaluation in

a broader sense (throughout or after the deliberative process) as opposed to *ex-ante* evaluation (assessing the opportunity to initiate a deliberative process in a specific situation).

How to use these guidelines

When conducting an evaluation using these guidelines, the aim is to assess a particular process and to use that evaluation to then improve the implementation of future deliberative processes. Evaluations use standard metrics (such as the member and organiser questionnaires) to gather reliable evidence and provide constructive feedback to commissioners and organisers, whether the overall evaluation is critical or positive.

These guidelines consist of three chapters. **Chapter 1** outlines five principles of evaluation and discusses key elements of planning and designing for evaluation. **Chapter 2** introduces the three-step evaluation cycle, framework, criteria, and measurement methods. **Chapter 3** opens the discussion on the wider impact and long-term effects, as well as evaluating institutionalised structures and processes for public deliberation.

These guidelines should be used by implementing the following four steps.

1. Decide on the principles and logistics (timing, resources, staffing) of the evaluation based on guidance provided in **Chapter 1** of the guidelines.
2. Set an evaluation framework, key criteria, and assessment methods based on guidance provided in **Chapter 2** of the guidelines.

2a. Building on the minimum evaluation guidelines

These guidelines provide a minimum set of evaluation criteria. They should be used as a foundation rather than as a comprehensive framework, and they should be adapted to the specific context in which the deliberative process is taking place. **Policy makers are encouraged to use these evaluation criteria in their entirety** and to add additional criteria based on their specific context and needs. This can be done by identifying specific evaluation needs via conversations with the public authorities commissioning the process and the practitioners implementing it.

2b. Taking into account the full participation strategy

When a deliberative process is part of a broader participation strategy on an issue, it is important to take into account that larger context. Evaluators can examine how the deliberative process fits into that strategy. For example, does the deliberation complement other participation efforts that aim to capture broader public opinion?

2c. Adapting the questionnaire included in these guidelines for your evaluation needs

These guidelines include two questionnaires. One is for members of a representative deliberative process, as part of the evaluation process. The other is for the process organisers.

3. Consider if it is feasible to evaluate long-term impacts, occurring over a relatively long period of time after the completion of a representative deliberative process. If applicable, adapt the evaluation framework to institutionalised structures and deliberative processes based on guidance provided in **Chapter 3** of the guidelines.
4. Find helpful resources and examples of good practice for evaluating representative deliberative processes in **Annex A: Further resources**.

Executive summary

These are guidelines for policy makers, evaluators, and practitioners who want to evaluate the representative deliberative processes they initiate, commission, and implement. The guidelines establish a minimum standard for evaluation by providing rationales, a framework, measurement methods, and evaluation questionnaires. The evaluation of deliberative processes is a key element of their success. Timely evaluation strengthens the trust of policy makers, the public, and stakeholders in recommendations developed by a deliberative body, as it can demonstrate the quality and the rigour involved in generating them. By making a process subject to evaluation, the authorities commissioning it demonstrate a commitment to transparency and quality, earning them greater legitimacy. Evaluation also creates opportunities for learning by providing evidence and lessons for public authorities and practitioners about what went well and what did not.

Independent evaluations are the most comprehensive and reliable way of evaluating a deliberative process. For smaller and shorter deliberative processes, evaluation in the form of self-reporting by members and/or organisers of a deliberative process can also contribute to learning. With the Advisory Group on Evaluating Representative Deliberative Processes, the OECD has developed principles that can help guide an evaluation and ensure its quality and integrity, summarised as follows:

- Maximum degree of independence of evaluation should be ensured, appropriate to the scale and length of a deliberative process.
- The selection of the evaluators and the evaluation process itself should be clear and transparent.
- Evaluations should be based on valid and reliable data, collected through a variety of methods, such as surveys, interviews, observation, and a review of materials used.
- Evaluators should have access to sufficient financial resources and all necessary information required to assess a deliberative process.
- The evaluation should be constructive and focus on quality and impact.

A comprehensive evaluation comprises three essential steps: evaluation of the process design integrity; the deliberative experience; and the pathways to impact of a deliberative process. Evaluation criteria has been identified for each step. Possible approaches and measurement methods to assess how a process meets the criteria include: member survey; public survey; organiser or expert witness survey; document review; deliberation observation; open-ended interviews; media coverage review, and policy analysis. Some evaluations consider wider impacts and long-term effects. The wider range of potential impacts includes changes to public attitudes and behaviour, long-run changes in the attitudes and behaviour of the deliberative process members, shifts in how public officials think and act, space created for civil society organisations, improved policy making, and changes in the logic of strategic actors in the political process.

It is highly recommended to evaluate the increasingly prevalent institutionalised structures and processes for public deliberation, as they are more durable, larger in scale, and potentially have a greater impact on decision making, the public, and policy makers. Additional evaluation criteria can be added to capture the ongoing nature of these processes.

1 Conducting an evaluation: Why, who, and how?

1.1 Why evaluate?

- The <u>OECD Good Practice Principles for Deliberative Processes for Public Decision Making</u> (2020a) recommend **evaluation of deliberative processes as a key element of a successful process.**
- Timely evaluation **strengthens the trust of policy makers, the public, and stakeholders in any recommendations developed by a deliberative body** as it can demonstrate the quality and the rigour involved in generating them. Each of these three groups, who were not part of the deliberative process, plays a role in implementing the deliberative body's recommendations. Their confidence in the legitimacy of the process is crucial.
- Evaluation can **demonstrate the level of quality and neutrality of a deliberative process.** When publicised, the results can increase trust in the deliberative process itself, as well as its resulting outputs that are used to inform public decision making. By making a process subject to evaluation, the authorities commissioning it demonstrate a commitment to transparency and quality, earning them greater legitimacy. Any groups that oppose the final recommendations of the deliberative body will scrutinise how its members reached their conclusions. Evaluation permits a clear sense of whether such critiques are justified.
- Evaluation also **creates opportunities for learning** by providing evidence and lessons for public authorities and practitioners about what went well and what did not. It gives a basis for iterative improvement.
- Evaluation **allows public authorities to identify which practitioners consistently deliver high-quality deliberative processes**, enhancing the accountability feedback loop

1.2 Evaluating representative deliberative processes

To date, evaluation of representative deliberative processes has been an emerging and fragmented practice. The 2020 OECD *Catching the Deliberative Wave* <u>report</u> found that the most common practice of evaluating representative deliberative process (67%) has been self-reporting by members of a deliberative process. Two per cent were found to have reflections by process organisers, although qualitative research shows that this number is likely to be much higher in reality. Seventeen per cent have had a research oriented academic analysis and only seven per cent have had an independent evaluation.

These guidelines recommend independent evaluations as a gold standard of evaluation, but recognise that it may not necessarily be feasible or appropriate for smaller scale, shorter deliberative processes due to time and budgetary constraints. In such cases, evaluation in the form of self-reporting by members and/or organisers of a deliberative process can also be a helpful practice for learning.

1.2.1 Independent evaluations

Independent evaluations are the most comprehensive and reliable way of evaluating a deliberative process. They are particularly valuable for deliberative processes that last a significant amount of time (e.g. four days or more).

Independent evaluators, ideally with training in evaluating deliberative processes, are best placed to provide an objective and fair assessment of a deliberative process. Independent evaluators can be external, in-house, or a mix of both. They are considered independent if they do not have any conflicts of interest regarding the policy issue, are not involved in designing or implementing the deliberative process, and are functionally independent from the people who are. Independent evaluators should have experience in evaluation methods, expertise in deliberative democracy, and an understanding of what a high-quality public deliberation entails.

Independent evaluations can use a range of methods. These often include observation of the process from start to finish, conducting member surveys, interviews, and assessment of informational material, whilst taking into account the reflections of the organising team and the facilitators. Please see **2.2 Measuring the Criteria** section of this document for further information.

1.2.2 Self-reporting by members of a deliberative process

Most evaluations of deliberative processes include confidential feedback from the members who have been selected via civic lottery. Their perspective is valuable as they personally experienced learning, deliberation, and decision making, and thus know what helped them complete their work, as well as what process features need improvement. However, as it is often the first deliberative process they have experienced, and their assessment is best used as part of broader evaluation by independent evaluators who are better placed to introduce a comparative perspective. The evaluation questions included in **Annex C** of these guidelines can elicit members' candid assessments of their deliberative process.

1.2.3 Hearing from organisers

In smaller and shorter deliberative processes, for example local-level processes that are one to three days long, evaluation and reflection often takes the form of self-reporting by the organising team. Organisers are the people who implemented a deliberative process, as opposed to those who commissioned it. They will have gained insights about what worked as intended and what challenges arose. They can also share creative solutions that they devised to address unexpected problems. Such feedback can help to improve future processes.

Organiser self-reporting often happens as an open discussion among team members or through a survey (when the evaluation is conducted by independent evaluators). **Annex D** of these guidelines provides evaluation questions for process organisers' surveys. **Annex E** provides evaluation questions for an open discussion between process organisers.

1.3 Five principles of evaluation

The following five principles have been developed by the OECD Advisory Group on Evaluating Representative Deliberative Processes. They can help guide an evaluation and ensure its quality and integrity.

1. **Independent:** For deliberative processes lasting a significant amount of time, evaluations should be impartial and thus independent. Independence entails being at arm's length from the commissioning public authority and the organisation implementing the process. The evaluators should have no stake in the outcome of the process and ideally have expertise in deliberation. For shorter, smaller-scale processes that are not evaluated by external evaluators, efforts should still be made to ensure a maximum degree of independence of evaluation.

2. **Transparent:** The selection of the evaluators should be clear and transparent. The evaluation process and the final evaluation report of a deliberative process should be made accessible and open to a peer review process. The evidence on which the evaluation is based should be published at an aggregate level, to the extent that it does not impede candid assessments or compromise confidentiality.

3. **Evidence-based:** Evaluations should be based on valid and reliable data. Evidence can be collected through a variety of methods, such as surveys, interviews, observation, and a review of materials used during a deliberative process. The standard measures in these guidelines should be used (see **Annex C**, **Annex D**, and **Annex E**).

4. **Accessible:** Evaluators should have access to sufficient financial resources and all necessary information required to assess a deliberative process, including recordings and controlled access to small group discussions. There should also be dedicated time in the programme for the evaluation team to access the members of a deliberative process for the purpose of filling in the evaluation survey(s), while ensuring that members are not burdened by such tasks and with due respect to the privacy and non-publicity of members' identities.

5. **Constructive:** A useful evaluation allows organisers and commissioning authorities to learn good practices and identify shortcomings to inform future processes. The evaluation should focus on the quality and impact of a deliberative process.

1.4 Planning and designing for evaluation

1.4.1 Ensuring an independent evaluation

- Independence of evaluations can be **structural and functional** (such as independence of the evaluation team with respect to the commissioners and organisers of the deliberative process) or **behavioural** (integrity and unbiasedness of the evaluators themselves) (OECD, 2020a). Efforts should be made to ensure independence in all of these regards.

- For large-scale processes, independence of the evaluation can be enhanced by setting up an evaluation oversight committee with external members, commitment to peer review, and declaration of absence of conflict of interest from the evaluators. Small-scale deliberative processes with very limited resources for evaluation should **at a minimum** use the standard measures and surveys in these guidelines – **Annex C**, **Annex D**, and **Annex E**.

- Ethical conduct of evaluators should be ensured (such as ethical use of data, research results, protection of members' privacy, confidentiality of responses).

- A credible evaluation needs **sufficient funding**, creating enough distance to ensure that the evaluation is independent, and that evaluators have sufficient access to the process.

- Funding for the evaluation can come from an independent, government funded institution. For example, The Scottish Citizens' Assembly evaluation was funded by Scottish Government Social Research. The process of awarding evaluative research of the Irish Citizens' Assembly was run by the Irish Research Council, with funding provided by the Department of An Taoiseach (Prime Minister).

- Academic institutions are often interested in partnering and are well-placed to provide credible and independent evaluations.

1.4.2 Planning for the timing and efficiency of an evaluation process

Planning for evaluation should take place during the design stage of a deliberative process. Commissioning the evaluators early will allow enough time to get everything started for the beginning of the process. The evaluation plan should be discussed with the commissioning authority and implementing practitioners to identify any areas of particular interest and ensure that all needs are met. While maintaining their independence, evaluators should seek to maximise the relevance of their report for practitioners, commissioners, stakeholders, and the public.

Organisers must reserve time in the programme for the evaluation team to conduct surveys and explain the importance of evaluation to the members. This ensures that the evaluators' access to the process is sufficient to properly do their job, whilst guaranteeing the highest possible response rates compared to post-process evaluation surveys. If there is no independent evaluation, it is still important to reserve this time so that organisers can both survey members and record their own assessments.

It is also helpful to agree to some fixed points in time after the deliberation when evaluators can revisit members of a deliberative process to obtain their views. Such follow-up contacts can help to assess long-term impacts and assessments of the broader process, such as whether the commissioning public authority responded constructively to the deliberative body's recommendations. Evaluators may also follow up with commissioning authorities to hear their perspectives on implementing the recommendations.

1.4.3. Resources needed for evaluation

Funding needed for evaluation should be considered from the start when commissioning a process.

1.5 Participatory evaluation

An evaluation can also include the members of a deliberative process and the broader public. Involving them creates an additional opportunity for public engagement, and potentially contributes to improving the quality of evaluations.

1.5.1 Members of a deliberative process

Members of a deliberative process can participate in evaluation process design, rather than only as subjects of the assessment. An evaluator can ask members what they perceive as the key criteria for a successful deliberative process. When done at the outset of an evaluation, such an exercise can help identify additional criteria for a comprehensive assessment.

An example of such evaluation is Healthy Democracy's emerging practice to set up a small committee of members with a mandate to design their own evaluation procedures. When given this opportunity, members have decided to set up daily feedback forms and designed an extensive survey to ask their fellow members about aspects of their experience.

1.5.2. The broader public

Members of the broader public could also serve as independent evaluators. Such members could be selected by a civic lottery to serve as evaluators, or they could volunteer to observe the process. Such initiatives would require dedicated resources to recruit people as evaluators and provide them with training and ensure independence. Expert evaluators or an academic partner would still be needed to help guide the process and ensure a comprehensive assessment. Ideally, an oversight committee with a mix of experts and members of the broader public could be set up to oversee the evaluation process and discuss the results.

1.6 Peer evaluation

Peer evaluation is an opportunity to invite expert witnesses, such as international deliberative democracy experts and practitioners or domestic peers (such as members of academia and NGOs), to observe a deliberative process. Peer observers can then provide an account of the process and be interviewed or surveyed to elicit relevant information for an evaluation. See **section 2.4 (measuring the evaluation criteria)** of this document for further details.

2 What to evaluate? Framework, criteria, and measurement methods

2.1. Three-Step evaluation cycle

A comprehensive evaluation comprises three essential steps: evaluation of the **process design integrity**; the **deliberative experience**; and the **pathways to impact** of a deliberative process. Together, these three steps allow an evaluator to have a full cycle view of a deliberative process.

Figure 2.1. Three-step evaluation cycle of a representative deliberative process

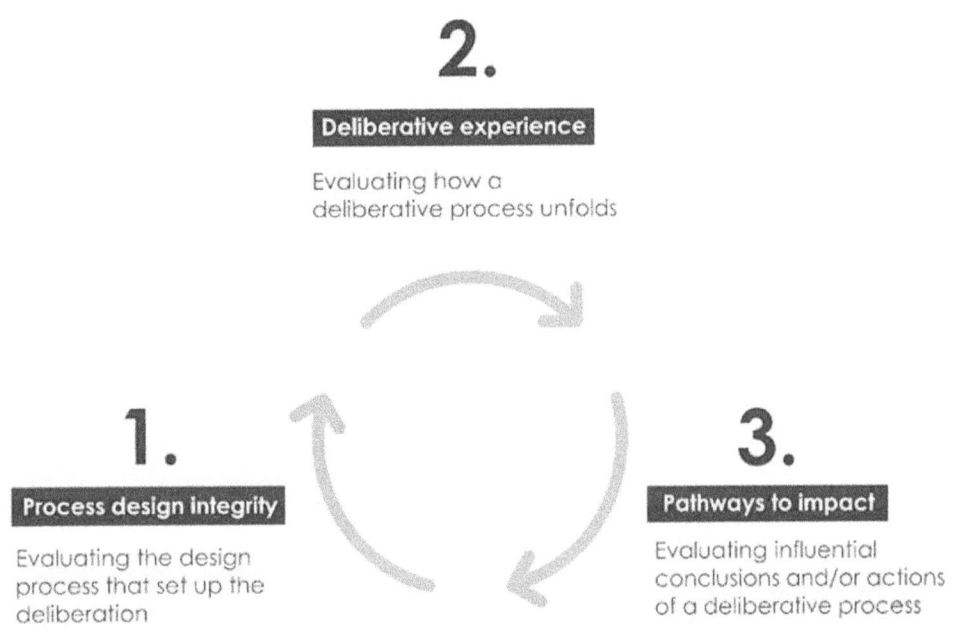

Source: Author's own creation

Process design integrity: Organisers frame the policy question and design a deliberative process before people gather in the room to deliberate. Evaluators will ask how these decisions were reached, whether the process has clear and legitimate objectives, whether the design choices are in line with those objectives, and whether the process design allows members enough time to learn and deliberate.

Deliberative experience: Once the deliberative process begins, everything that happens "in the room" and "outside the room" is important. These include the breadth, diversity, and clarity of the evidence and stakeholders presented, the quality of facilitation, opportunities to speak, removal of participation barriers, as well as mitigation of undesired attention and/or attempts at interference.

Pathways to impact: Once a deliberative process is completed and recommendations have been produced, the spotlight turns to the uptake of those recommendations by the commissioning body. Responses and justifications are expected for all recommendations. Depending on the type of deliberative process, it may be necessary to measure its uptake by the broader public (for example, when it is followed by a referendum).

2.2 Framework

The following table sets out the evaluation framework based on the three steps of the evaluation cycle and provides an overview of the key criteria for evaluating each of them.

Table 2.1. Framework for evaluating a representative deliberative process

	Process evaluation		Outcome evaluation
	Process design integrity	**Deliberative experience**	**Pathways to impact**
Objective	Evaluating the design process that set up the deliberation	Evaluating how a deliberative process unfolds "in the room" and "outside the room"	Evaluating influential conclusions and/or actions of a deliberative process
Criteria	<ul><li>Clear and suitable purpose</li><li>Clear and unbiased framing</li><li>Suitable design</li><li>Procedural design involvement</li><li>Transparency and governance</li><li>Representativeness and inclusiveness</li></ul>	<ul><li>Neutrality and inclusivity of facilitation</li><li>Accessible, neutral, and transparent use of online tools</li><li>Breadth, diversity, clarity and relevance of the evidence and stakeholders</li><li>Quality of judgement</li><li>Perceived knowledge gains by members</li><li>Accessibility and equality of opportunity to speak</li><li>Respect and mutual comprehension</li><li>Free decision-making and response</li><li>Respect for members' privacy</li></ul>	<ul><li>Influential recommendations</li><li>Response and follow-up</li><li>Member aftercare</li></ul>

Source: Author's own creation

2.3 Evaluation criteria

The evaluation criteria outlined in the framework are detailed below:

1) Process design integrity

Clear and suitable purpose

- The deliberative process was commissioned for a suitable purpose, addressing a policy issue. (See *Catching the Deliberative Wave* report (OECD, 2020a) Chapter 4 section *Scope of the remit* for guidance.)
- The mandate was clear and it was clear how the recommendations will be used.
- The deliberative process was connected to the broader political system or policy-making cycle.

Clear and unbiased framing

The question addressed by the deliberative process was framed in a non-leading, unbiased, clear way, easily understandable to the wider public.

Suitable design

- The design choices of a deliberative process were aligned with its objectives.

- The resulting process was in line with *OECD Good Practice Principles*, see **Annex B**. For example, sufficient length of the process, group deliberation, etc.

Procedural design involvement

- Organisers had an established process to call for, respond to, and recognise comments from stakeholders regarding the deliberative process design.
- A wide range of stakeholders representing diverse views had an opportunity to review the deliberative process design.
- Experts in the policy area were consulted over the questions and the choice of evidence provided.
- Deliberative democracy experts (in-house or external) were consulted on process design.

Transparency and governance

- There were clear terms of reference, rules of engagement, codes of conduct, or ethical frameworks that govern the process. They were followed throughout the process.
- Information about the goals, design, governance of the process, funding source, civic lottery, and any other materials were published publicly.
- The design of the process was free of external interference.

Representativeness and inclusiveness

- Everyone had an equal opportunity, via civic lottery, to be selected as a member of a deliberative process. (For example, all residents or eligible voters.)
- The final group of members was a broadly representative sample of the general public (reflecting the demographic composition of a community, city, region, or country). (Anyone looking at the members could see 'someone like me' within the process.)
- Efforts were made to involve under-represented groups. (In some instances, it is desirable to over-sample certain demographics during the random sampling stage of recruitment to help achieve representativeness.)
- Efforts were made to remove barriers to participation. The *OECD Good Practice Principles* identify remuneration of the members, covering their expenses, and/or providing or paying for childcare and eldercare as helpful ways to encourage and support participation.

2) Deliberative experience

Neutrality and inclusivity of facilitation

- The facilitation ensured inclusiveness, equal access to speaking opportunities, and appropriate balance of small group and panel discussions throughout deliberation.
- Enough consideration was given for marginalised communities to be heard. (For example, via supportive and mindful facilitation, creating a safe space for expression, devising specific strategies for encouraging participation by those who are not used to speaking in public or who may feel intimidated.)
- Facilitation was neutral regarding the issue addressed.

Accessible, neutral, and transparent use of online tools

- Any online tools used throughout the process were equally accessible to all members. There was assistance, training, equipment, and internet connection offered and/or provided. (For some

members who are unfamiliar with the internet or online tools, it may be necessary to have one-on-one support during the process.)
- The design of the online tools used was neutral and transparent (for example, the algorithms or formulas used for preference or vote counting were explicit and clear, online tools ensured anonymity of members when needed, and the results calculated/aggregated using online tools were auditable).

Breadth, diversity, clarity, and relevance of the evidence and stakeholders provided

- Members were provided a solid and accessible information base featuring a wide range of accurate relevant, clear and accessible evidence and expertise, sufficient for effective participation and to address the remit set.
- The information base as a whole was neutral, with a breadth of diverse viewpoints represented. (Ensured, for example, through mapping all the arguments of the issue with stakeholders to see whether all relevant areas and viewpoints are reflected in the information base.)
- The information base was accommodating to members with different learning styles and included materials in a variety of forms (written, video, in-person expert presentations etc.).
- There was a wide range of stakeholder views. (This could include an element of public submission.)
- The selection of sources was transparent, revealing the curator and the basis for selecting the content. People in charge of preparing the information base had declared any potential conflict of interest.
- Members had a possibility to submit evidence for consideration and request additional information.

Quality of judgement

- There was consideration of conflicting values and structural issues underlying the question at hand.
- There was an emphasis on diversity of viewpoints, weighing of alternatives and trade-offs, exploring uncertainties, and exposing assumptions.
- Members provided justifications for their viewpoints.
- Members approached the process with open-mindedness.
- Members considered and integrated range of evidence in their judgements.

Perceived knowledge gains by members

- Members have exercised and gained empathy by developing mutual understanding and considering different views and experiences.
- Members have gained a clearer understanding of each other's opinions.
- After deliberation, members have a better understanding of both the policy issue and the public decision-making process in general.
- The opinion of each member became clearer through deliberation and moved towards informed judgement.

Accessibility and equality of opportunity to speak

- All members had equal speaking opportunities, opportunity to influence the discussions, and equal access to any necessary support, tools, or resources during the process.
- Members had the opportunity to provide ongoing feedback and suggest modifications of the process (such as asking for more time or reporting experienced bias).

Respect and mutual comprehension

- Interactions amongst members were respectful.
- There was careful and active listening, as well as interactive deliberation that allowed members to weigh each other's views.
- All members felt heard in the process.

Free decision making and response

- The implementation of the process was free of interference beyond set roles and processes (i.e. intrusions by experts, steering group members).
- The final recommendations represent what the members actually think (i.e. members had a final say over the wording of the recommendations).
- The final decision making was non-coercive, using democratic decision-making rules (i.e. consensus, majority rule, ranking etc.).
- The report fully reflects the judgement of the group, including views that were not supported by the majority. Members were free and supported to contribute a minority report which appears in the appendix to the main report.

Respect for members' privacy

- Members' privacy was protected. For more details, see **Annex B** – *Principle 10: Privacy*.
- There was no undesired attention or attempt at interference from the media, stakeholders, or other actors.

3) Pathways to impact

Influential recommendations

- The commissioners of the process identified and pursued a set of plausible pathways to immediate policy impact.
- The impact (influential conclusions and/or actions) of the deliberative process corresponds to the mandate it was given.
- The report of the deliberative process was released publicly.
- Efforts were made to disseminate the report widely.
- The members' recommendations had an opportunity to influence opinions and decisions made by a commissioning body, other public institutions, or the broader public.

Response and follow-up

- The government or equivalent commissioning body responded to members of the deliberative process and/or to the general public. (Ideally, such a body would accept the recommendations or provide a public justification for why not.)
- The implementation of all accepted recommendations was monitored with regular public progress reports.

Member aftercare

- The members of the deliberative process were provided information on how to follow the uptake of their recommendations and further engage in the policy-making process.

- The members had necessary support to speak about their experiences and recommendations to their communities or the broader public.
- Communication channels were established for members to maintain their connection amongst themselves after the deliberative process.

2.4 Measuring the evaluation criteria

There are different ways that evaluators can assess how a deliberative process meets the criteria outlined above. It is important to balance subjective and objective measures when evaluating, to help maintain objectivity. This section covers possible approaches and methods to measure the evaluation criteria for each of the three steps of the evaluation cycle.

Table 2.2. Overview of the applicability of measurement methods for assessing evaluation criteria

Step	Criteria	Member survey	Public survey	Organiser or expert witness survey	Document review	Deliberation observation	Open-ended Interviews	Media coverage review	Policy analysis
Process design integrity	Clear and suitable purpose		X	X	X		X		
	Clear and unbiased framing	X	X	X	X				
	Suitable design	X			X	X			
	Procedural design involvement		X		X	X	X		
	Transparency and governance	X	X	X	X		X	X	
	Representativeness and inclusiveness	X	X	X	X				
Deliberative experience	Neutrality, inclusivity, and balance of facilitation	X		X	X	X	X		
	Accessible, neutral, and transparent use of online tools	X		X	X	X	X		
	Breadth, diversity, clarity, and relevance of the evidence and stakeholders	X			X	X	X		
	Quality of judgement	X		X		X	X		
	Perceived knowledge gains by members	X		X		X	X		
	Accessibility and equality of opportunity to speak	X				X	X		
	Respect and mutual comprehension	X		X		X	X		
	Free decision-making and response	X		X	X	X	X		
	Respect for members' privacy	X		X	X	X	X		
Pathways to impact	Influential recommendations	X						X	X
	Response and follow up	X	X		X		X	X	X
	Member aftercare			X	X		X		

Source: Author's own creation

Member survey

Surveying the members of a deliberative process with a standard evaluation survey is a recommended minimum measurement method to evaluate some elements of **process design integrity** and all elements of the **deliberative experience**. Annex C contains an evaluation questionnaire that should be used to elicit relevant information from members at the end of the process. It is important to ensure that members of the deliberative process are able to answer the questionnaire confidentially to ensure honesty and openness.

Public survey

A public survey can also be a helpful to evaluate some elements of evaluating **impact**, such as government response or the awareness about the deliberative process amongst the broader public. It can also help assess elements of **process design integrity**, such as the clarity of purpose and framing and transparency.

Organiser or expert witness survey

The organiser survey can complement the answers provided by members of the deliberative process and provide insights from the perspective of people who have previously organised deliberative processes and can compare it to their prior experiences. As process organisers and facilitators, they also interact with the commissioning body and have insights into not only the **deliberative experience** but also the **process design**. Annex D contains an evaluation questionnaire that can be used to elicit relevant information from organisers. These questions can be used as a survey, or as guidance for a collective self-evaluation and reflection session. If expert witnesses are present in the process, they can also be asked most of these questions.

Document review

Document review is a method that helps to gather objective information about a deliberative process and can be put to good use to help validate some of the more perception-based information sources, such as surveys and interviews. Evaluating **process design integrity** relies heavily on document review. For example, evaluating representativeness of the panel by comparing member demographics with census data, evaluating transparency by verifying the availability of various documents to the public, evaluating suitable design of a deliberative process by examining the timeline, the agenda, and the various stages of a deliberative process.

Some elements of the **deliberative experience** can also be evaluated in this way, such as the evidence base presented to the members to evaluate its breadth and diversity, any online tools, or the final set of member recommendations. Transcripts of the deliberation can also be reviewed to evaluate the amount of time that members of different groups take in speaking.

Evidence review is also crucial for evaluating **impact** – such as assessing the commissioning authority's response and follow-up to the members.

Deliberation observation

Observation is essential to evaluate the **deliberative experience** of the process. By having access to the sessions, evaluators can form a judgement of how each of the criteria was met. This is especially important for criteria such as equal opportunity to speak, respect amongst the members, and quality of judgement.

However, it is important to ensure that there are not too many observers, especially during small group discussions, and that they do not interfere in any way with the process.

Open-ended interviews

Qualitative interviews with representatives of the commissioning authority, relevant stakeholders, policy makers, expert witnesses, journalists, or members is another useful method to complement evaluation efforts. Interviews with policy makers can be helpful for identifying the extent that members' recommendations were influential. Interviews with stakeholders can shed light on the openness and transparency of the deliberative process design. Interviewing the commissioning body can be helpful in identifying the motivations behind the initiation of a deliberative process. Interviews with a selection of members can provide additional insights to the quantitative survey results.

Media coverage review

Reviewing media coverage of the deliberative process, along with coverage of the policy issue addressed, can be useful in evaluating the extent of influence the process had on both the public decision-making process and the broader public. Changes in the discourse around, in the framings of, and the popularity of the policy issue on traditional media outlets or social media can indicate public perception and provide details on government response to recommendations. Media coverage review is most useful for evaluating **pathways to impact**.

Policy analysis

Policy analysis also helps in evaluating **pathways to impact.** Sometimes it can be difficult to attribute policy changes to deliberative processes, but other times those links can be clear. Identifying these links can help highlight the value of the deliberative process to public decision making. Policy analysis can include document review and interviews with stakeholders and policy makers. It can also be comparative, looking at relevant changes in policy, legislation, and/or institutional structures before and after a deliberative process takes place.

3 Going beyond: Building on the minimum criteria

3.1 Wider impact and long-term effects

In addition to the criteria outlined in the previous section to evaluate the full cycle of a deliberative process, some evaluations consider potential wider impacts and long-term effects. Such evaluations take into account long-term changes in the attitudes and behaviours of members of deliberative processes, public officials, and/or the broader public over a longer period of time. As the focus of these guidelines is the minimum evaluation standards, detailed in **Chapter 2** of this document, this section merely opens the discussion on evaluating wider impact and long term-effects, which is still an emerging practice.

To avoid delays in publishing the evaluation of the full cycle of a deliberative process, the wider impact and long-term evaluation report should be published at a later date as a separate document.

Evaluating broader impacts and long-term effects of deliberative processes gives a clearer estimate of the long-term value of public involvement in policy making. However, it requires additional time and financial resources, and proving causal effects presents additional challenges for evaluators.

Evaluating wider impact and long-term effects can be particularly useful when several deliberative processes have a cumulative impact, when the deliberative processes are large-scale and high-profile, and when structures and processes for public deliberation are ongoing.

The wider range of potential impacts includes changes to public attitudes and behaviour, long-run changes in the attitudes and behaviour of the deliberative process members, shifts in how public officials think and act, space created for civil society organisations, improved policy making, and changes in the logic of strategic actors in the political process.

Effects on the public

- Stable or rising levels of public trust in government
- Potential increase of voter turnout in elections
- Increased sense of political self-confidence

Empowering the members of deliberative process

- Increased democratic capacities (for example, self-expression, empathy, deliberation skills)
- Strengthened political knowledge and interest
- Increased open-mindedness and ability to appreciate complexity of perspectives

Effects on public officials and public bodies

- Serious consideration of and engagement with the recommendations given by members of deliberative processes
- Recognising the value of inviting everyday people to deliberate before reaching policy judgements
- Seeing a role for public deliberation in the policy-making process
- Increasing the uptake of deliberative processes

Creating space for civil society organisations

- Civil society organisations granted opportunities of access to a deliberative process to provide feedback on the design of the process, contribute with evidence and expertise

- Levelling the playing field and enhancing transparency and accountability of public, private, and civil society stakeholder influence on public decisions as undue influence on a public decisions is mitigated via deliberative processes

Improving policy making (policy formulation, implementation, outcomes)

- Policy outputs become more aligned with informed public judgement
- Wider range of voices heard in policy making
- Fewer policy failures due to more accurate policy responses
- More polarising issues addressed in respectful ways

Altering political strategy

- Issues raised by deliberative panels influence future legislative priorities and issue campaigns
- Stakeholder groups and public officials develop or test potential policy initiatives with deliberative processes to improve the quality of such proposals from the outset

Evaluation of these criteria can be done by employing the methods of interviews with public officials and members of a deliberative process, as well as longitudinal population surveys.

Annex A: Further resources provides more information on impact and long-term effect evaluation of deliberative processes.

Box 1. Examples: Assessing wider impact and long-term effects

Strengthened political knowledge and interest

Two case studies of representative deliberative processes, the Australian Citizens' Parliament and Italy's Iniziativa di Revisione Civica, were analysed to uncover the relationship between the process and the wider system and its deliberative capacity. The results show that these case studies have encouraged wider use of deliberative processes over the long term. Former members of a deliberative process have shown increased interest in political life and engagement in it. Public authorities were also inclined to promote the use of deliberative processes in the future by establishing a fund to further finance subsequent citizens' participation councils.

Source: Felicetti, A., Niemeyer, S., & Curato, N. (2016). Improving deliberative participation: Connecting mini-publics to deliberative systems. *European Political Science Review*, 8(3), 427–448. https://doi.org/10.1017/S1755773915000119

Increased sense of political self-confidence

A two-wave panel survey of registered Oregon voters in 2010 and a second 2012 survey of registered Oregon voters were employed to investigate whether a Citizens' Initiative Review (CIR) process in Oregon had an impact on the wider public. Results demonstrate that deliberative processes can support positive political attitudes among the members of the process, such as increased political efficacy, confidence in themselves and in democratic institutions. Similar effects were observed amongst the wider public, especially those who most utilise the published findings of the process. Knowing about the CIR taking place increased respondents' external efficacy (belief in responsiveness of the government to citizens' needs). Whereas those respondents who have read or even used the findings of the CIR felt an increase in internal efficacy (belief in their capacity to effectively participate in political life).

Source: Knobloch, K. R., Barthel, M., & Gastil, J. (2019). Emanating effects: The impact of the Oregon Citizens' Initiative Review on voters' political efficacy. *Political Studies*, 68, 426-445. https://doi.org/10.1177/0032321719852254

3.2 Evaluating institutionalised structures and processes for public deliberation

The OECD Catching the Deliberative Wave report (2020) found that public authorities are increasingly looking for ways to make representative deliberative processes a more permanent and ongoing part of governance. The OECD guide *Eight Ways to Institutionalise Deliberative Democracy* (2021) has identified eight models for embedding public deliberation and civic lotteries in existing democratic institutions.

It is highly recommended to evaluate institutionalised structures and processes for public deliberation, as they are longer-term, larger-scale, and potentially have a bigger impact on decision-making, the public, and policymakers. Learning what works well and what requires improvement also allows for refinement and adaptation.

Overall, the criteria outlined in these guidelines are equally applicable to the evaluation of ongoing structures and processes for public deliberation. Some additional criteria can be added to capture the ongoing nature of these processes. Broadly, institutionalised structures and processes for public deliberation can be split in two groups:

1. **Permanent or ongoing structures for representative citizen deliberation**, such as within or adjoining the parliament or government. Such structures often have an agenda-setting power.
2. ***Ad hoc* structures required in certain conditions**, such as after a demand from the public, if a public decision is connected to a certain policy area, or requiring a specific threshold of spending. These processes are more demand-driven and dispersed in time and location, but are anchored in legislation or regulation that typically sets out the parameters and criteria for their establishment and implementation.

Keeping these differences in mind, there are additional criteria to consider when evaluating ongoing structures and processes for public deliberation.

Agenda-setting power

- All members of a particular group (the public/politicians/policy makers) have equal access to the possibility to initiate a deliberative process.
- Members of the public/policy makers/politicians have taken the opportunity to initiate a deliberative process.

Regularity and coherence

- Deliberative processes conform to the same standards across different instances/places/circumstances.
- Deliberative processes are initiated regularly.

Learning and capacity

- Learning mechanisms are in place to allow the commissioners/organisers of a deliberative process to pass on their lessons and experience to others organising such a process in the future.
- Guidance/training/support on the use of deliberative processes is provided when there are requirements to conduct deliberative processes under certain circumstances.

Rotation and retention

- In cases of a permanent or ongoing structure for representative citizen deliberation, the attrition rate of the members of the permanent body is low.
- When appropriate, an adequate and effective mechanism of rotation is provided for the members of the permanent body.

Annex A. Further information resources

Representative deliberative processes
- OECD (2020a), *Innovative Citizen Participation and New Democratic Institutions: Catching the Deliberative Wave*, https://doi.org/10.1787/339306da-en.
- OECD (2021), Eight Ways to Institutionalise Deliberative Democracy, OECD Publishing, Paris.
- UN Democracy Fund and newDemocracy Foundation (2019) *Handbook on Democracy Beyond Elections*.

Impact and long-term effect evaluation
- Gastil, J., Knobloch, K., Reedy, J., Henkels, M., & Cramer, K. (2018). Assessing the electoral impact of the 2010 Oregon Citizens' Initiative Review. *American Politics Research*, 46, 534–563.
- Knobloch, K. R., Barthel, M., & Gastil, J. (2019). Emanating effects: The impact of the Oregon Citizens' Initiative Review on voters' political efficacy. *Political Studies*, 68, 426-445. https://doi.org/10.1177/0032321719852254
- Felicetti, A., Niemeyer, S., & Curato, N. (2016). Improving deliberative participation: Connecting mini-publics to deliberative systems. *European Political Science Review*, 8(3), 427–448. https://doi.org/10.1017/S1755773915000119
- Goodin, R. E., & Dryzek, J. S. (2006). Deliberative Impacts: The Macro-Political Uptake of Mini-Publics. *Politics & Society*, 34(2), 219–244. https://doi.org/10.1177/0032329206288152
- Jacquet, V., & Does, R. van der. (2020). The Consequences of Deliberative Minipublics: Systematic Overview, Conceptual Gaps, and New Directions. *Representation*, 0(0), 1–11. https://doi.org/10.1080/00344893.2020.1778513

Examples of evaluation of representative deliberative process

Please note that examples below are not examples of evaluations done following the guidelines outlined in this document. Nevertheless, they can be a helpful starting point.

- Evaluations of Citizens' Initiative Review processes
- Evaluation of the Scottish Parliament's Citizens' Panels on Primary Care
- Evaluation of Climate Assembly UK
- Evaluation of Buergerrat Demokratie (in german)
- Democracy Matters: Lessons from the 2015 Citizens' Assemblies on English Devolution
- Evaluation Report of the Irish Citizens' Assembly on Gender Equality

Policy evaluation
- OECD (2020b), *Improving Governance with Policy Evaluation : Lessons From Country Experiences*, https://doi.org/10.1787/89b1577d-en

Annex B. OECD Good practice principles for deliberative processes for public decision making

Based on analysis of the data collected and in collaboration with an advisory group of leading practitioners from government, civil society, and academia, the OECD has identified common principles and good practices that may be of useful guidance to policy makers seeking to develop and implement representative deliberative processes. See Chapter 5 of the *Catching the Deliberative Wave* report (OECD, 2020a) for more details on the methodology and context.

1. **Purpose:** The objective should be outlined as a clear task and is linked to a defined public problem. It is phrased neutrally as a question in plain language.
2. **Accountability:** There should be influence on public decisions. The commissioning public authority should publicly commit to responding to or acting on participants' recommendations in a timely manner. It should monitor the implementation of all accepted recommendations with regular public progress reports.
3. **Transparency:** The deliberative process should be announced publicly before it begins. The process design and all materials – including agendas, briefing documents, evidence submissions, audio and video recordings of those presenting evidence, the participants' report, their recommendations (the wording of which participants should have a final say over), and the random selection methodology – should be available to the public in a timely manner. The funding source should be disclosed. The commissioning public authority's response to the recommendations and the evaluation after the process should be publicised and have a public communication strategy.
4. **Representativeness:** The participants should be a microcosm of the general public. This is achieved through random sampling from which a representative selection is made, based on stratification by demographics (to ensure the group broadly matches the demographic profile of the community against census or other similar data), and sometimes by attitudinal context (depending on the context). Everyone should have an equal opportunity to be selected as participants. In some instances, it may be desirable to over-sample certain demographics during the random sampling stage of recruitment to help achieve representativeness.
5. **Inclusiveness:** Inclusion should be achieved by considering how to involve under-represented groups. Participation should also be encouraged and supported through remuneration, expenses, and/or providing or paying for childcare and eldercare.
6. **Information:** Participants should have access to a wide range of accurate, relevant, and accessible evidence and expertise. They should have the opportunity to hear from and question speakers that present to them, including experts and advocates chosen by the citizens themselves.

7. **Group deliberation:** Participants should be able to find common ground to underpin their collective recommendations to the public authority. This entails careful and active listening, weighing and considering multiple perspectives, every participant having an opportunity to speak, a mix of formats that alternate between small group and plenary discussions and activities, and skilled facilitation.

8. **Time:** Deliberation requires adequate time for participants to learn, weigh the evidence, and develop informed recommendations, due to the complexity of most policy problems. To achieve informed citizen recommendations, participants should meet for at least four full days in person, unless a shorter time frame can be justified. It is recommended to allow time for individual learning and reflection in between meetings.

9. **Integrity:** The process should be run by an arms' length co-ordinating team different from the commissioning public authority. The final call regarding process decisions should be with the arms' length co-ordinators rather than the commissioning authorities. Depending on the context, there should be oversight by an advisory or monitoring board with representatives of different viewpoints.

10. **Privacy:** There should be respect for participants' privacy to protect them from undesired media attention and harassment, as well as to preserve participants' independence, ensuring they are not bribed or lobbied by interest groups or activists. Small group discussions should be private. The identity of participants may be publicised when the process has ended, at the participants' consent. All personal data of participants should be treated in compliance with international good practices, such as the European Union's General Data Protection Regulation (GDPR).

11. **Evaluation:** There should be an anonymous evaluation by the participants to assess the process based on objective criteria (e.g. on quantity and diversity of information provided, amount of time devoted to learning, independence of facilitation). An internal evaluation by the co-ordination team should be conducted against the good practice principles in this report to assess what has been achieved and how to improve future practice. An independent evaluation is recommended for some deliberative processes, particularly those that last a significant time. The deliberative process should also be evaluated on final outcomes and impact of implement recommendations.

Annex C. Member questionnaire

The following questionnaire is for the members of the deliberative body to respond to at the end of the process. Some of the questions could be asked both at the beginning and at the end of the process. These are marked with a symbol **X2**.

For longer, larger-scale deliberative processes it is recommended that all questions are included as a minimum evaluation. For smaller, shorter processes where administering the full questionnaire is not feasible, some questions could be omitted if less relevant. It is highly encouraged to keep the exact wording of the questions, as they have been designed following survey-writing standards to be non-leading and fair. Keeping the exact question wording also allows for comparability of evaluation results across the field.

To ensure they are non-leading, these questions should be included in a survey *without* headlines. Response options should be provided in a randomised order, where indicated.

It can be helpful to introduce a few demographic questions at the outset of the survey, such as gender, age, and some form of socioeconomic criteria. Answers to the survey should be confidential and members should have the right not to answer any questions. Survey results should be public, but analysed in aggregate, protecting individual responses.

This questionnaire was designed in consultation with the Expert Advisory group on Evaluating Representative Deliberative Processes, the Innovative Citizen Participation Network and the Democracy R&D Network. It was also informed by a comparative analysis of existing questionnaires designed for a similar purpose. As this is a new questionnaire yet to be tested in different contexts, we are interested in receiving feedback from those using it. Based on this feedback, an updated version of this questionnaire will be published.

1) Process design integrity

Clear and unbiased framing

1. Please describe the task you and other members were given in your own words. **X2**

2. Does the outcome of the deliberative process (such as the quality of the recommendations) match the expectations you had about this process when you received the initial invitation? Please explain.

3. To what extent, if at all, do you think that the task you were given allowed you to consider a narrow or a wide range of options for your recommendations? Please answer on a scale of 0 to 10, where 0 is "extremely narrow", 5 is "just right" and 10 is "extremely wide".

Suitable design

4. Do you think the length of the process was appropriate?
    a) Yes

b) No, I think the amount of time was just right
c) No, I thought the process was too long
d) I'm not sure

5. If you consider the process needed more time, how much extra time do you think would have been useful?
    a) Just a little bit more – a half day or less
    b) At least one full day of deliberation
    c) At least two-three more days of deliberation
    d) A lot more time would have been useful – four days or more of deliberation

6. If you consider the process needed more time, how would you use the extra time? Please choose all relevant options. (randomised response order)
    a) Hearing from more experts
    b) Hearing from more stakeholders
    c) Deliberating and weighing the different arguments before developing our recommendations
    d) Developing our recommendations
    e) Agreeing on the final wording of our recommendations
    f) Having more/longer breaks
    g) Other – please explain

7. To what extent, if at all, do you think that the time you had was well used to arrive at the final recommendations? Please answer on a scale of 0 to 10, where 0 means "not at all" and 10 means "extremely well used".

8. Would it have been possible for you to have given more time to this process?
    a) Yes
    b) No

Transparency and governance

9. What is your understanding of what will happen next with the recommendations you will work on/were working on? X2

Representativeness and inclusiveness

10. How many of the other members did you feel had different views compared to your own?
    a) None
    b) A few of them
    c) About half of them
    d) Most of them
    e) I don't know

11. Did you feel there were any groups or parts of society that were not represented on this panel?
    a) Yes
    b) No

12. If you feel any groups or parts of society were not represented, which group or groups did you feel was/were missing?

13. Were there any obstacles that made it difficult for you to attend the sessions?
    a) Yes
    b) No

14. If there were obstacles that made it difficult for you to attend, what were they? Tick all that apply. (randomised response order for options a-e)
    a) Barriers related to my personal life (for example, family commitments)
    b) Barriers related to my work (for example, irregular working hours, busy schedule)
    c) Financial barriers (for example, travelling costs)
    d) The time this process demands
    e) Yes, other barriers (please specify)
    f) I don't know

15. Do you have any suggestions of what could be done to improve the ability for anyone to attend such a process?

2) Deliberative experience

Neutrality and inclusivity of facilitation

16. How did you experience the balance between time spent in small group discussions and in plenary (whole group discussions) throughout the process? (randomised response order)
    a) Too much time spent in small groups, not enough in plenary
    b) Too much time spent in plenary, not enough in small groups
    c) The balance between small groups and plenary was just right

17. To what extent did you feel that the facilitators were neutral or biased (favouring certain opinions or offering theirs)? Please answer on a scale of 0 to 10, where 0 means "completely neutral" and 10 means "very biased".

Accessible, neutral, and transparent use of online tools

18. [If online tools used] To what extent did you find the online tools, such as [indicate the tool used] easy or difficult to use? Please answer on a scale of 0 to 10, where 0 is "very difficult" and 10 is "very easy".

19. Did you receive sufficient technical support and equipment, if needed?
    a) Yes, I received all the technical support and equipment I needed
    b) Yes, I received some technical support and equipment but did not feel entirely supported
    c) No, I felt I did not receive the technical support or equipment that I needed
    d) I did not need technical support or equipment

20. Did you find that the online tools used did, or did not, were helpful to the process?
    a) Yes
    b) No

Breadth, diversity, clarity, and relevance of the evidence and stakeholders

21. To what extent do you feel that the information resources provided to you to help discussions were narrow or broad? Please answer on a scale of 0 to 10, where 0 means "the information provided was too narrow", 5 means "the breadth of information provided was just right" and 10 means "the information provided was too broad".

22. To what extent do you feel that the information resources provided, as a whole, neutral, with fair and diverse viewpoints represented? Please answer on a scale of 0 to 10, where 0 means "the information base felt very biased" and 10 means "the information base felt neutral with a large diversity of sources".

23. Would you have liked to request presentations from additional experts or stakeholders beyond those lined up by the steering committee?
    a) Yes
    b) No
    c) I did request presentations from additional experts

24. If you did request presentations from additional experts or stakeholders, were they called?
    a) Yes, all additional experts requested were called
    b) Yes, but only some of the additional experts requested were called
    c) No, they were not called

25. If requested expert(s) could not attend, were you satisfied with the alternative expert(s)?
    a) Yes
    b) No

26. Were you able to request and obtain additional information beyond that which was initially provided to you by the organisers?
    a) Yes, requested additional information, and it was provided
    b) Yes, requested additional information, but it was not provided

c) Yes, we could request additional information, but we did not feel we needed any
d) No, we were not able to request additional information
e) I don't know if we were able to request additional information

27. Did you find the evidence that was presented by the speakers easy or hard to understand?
    a) I understood it easily from the beginning
    b) Initially it was hard to understand, but by the end of the process I understood a lot of it much better
    c) I found all of it hard to understand throughout
    d) I don't know

Quality of judgement

28. To what extent, if at all, do you feel that the final recommendations reflected the different views and judgements of the members? Please answer on a scale of 0 to 10, where 0 means "the diversity was not at all reflected" and 10 means "ultimately, our recommendations broadly satisfied the concerns of all members".

29. To what extent, if at all, do you feel that the issue was discussed from a variety of perspectives (for example, considering underlying issues, existing structures, trade-offs values etc.)? Please answer on a scale of 0 to 10, where 0 means "from very limited number of perspectives" and 10 means "the issue was discussed from a wide variety of perspectives".

30. To what extent do you feel that most members were providing justifications and explanations for their opinions? Please answer on a scale of 0 to 10, where 0 means "most members never provided justifications and explanations" and 10 means "most members always provided justifications and explanations".

Perceived knowledge gains by members

Note: In addition to the questions below, knowledge gains can also be tested by asking a few factual questions about the policy issue that members tackled. Factual questions should be asked in the beginning and at the end of a deliberative process, in order to observe changes in the number of right answers.

Please answer all of the following questions on a scale of 0 to 10, where 0 means "not at all" and 10 means "to a great extent". To what extent, if at all, do you feel that:

31. your understanding of the issue became clearer throughout the process?
32. you gained more arguments and perspectives to support your own opinion about the issue?
33. you understood the arguments, perspectives, and concerns of others?
34. your understanding of others' opinions of the issue became clearer through this process?

35. On a scale of 0 to 10, where 0 means "not at all informed" and 10 means "very well informed", to what extent, if at all, do you feel that you are informed at the moment on

the following issues: (include a list of issues relevant to the key policy issue addressed) **X2 (or more)**

Accessibility and equality of opportunity to speak

Please answer all of the following questions on a scale of 0 to 10, where 0 means "not at all" and 10 means "to a great extent". To what extent, if at all, do you feel that:

36. you had a fair number of opportunities to speak?
37. other members had a fair number of opportunities to speak?
38. all members were heard equally?
39. no members dominated the discussions?
40. you and your views were heard?

Respect and mutual comprehension

41. fellow members respected what you had to say, even when they didn't agree with you?

Free decision making and response

42. organisers, experts, or steering group members expressed their own views during members' deliberation?
43. Imagine you are the decision-maker that convened this process. Would you implement the recommendations the deliberative process produced?
    a) Yes, all of them
    b) Yes, the vast majority (over 75%)
    c) Yes, about half
    d) Yes, some (between 25-50%)
    e) Only a few (between 1-25%)
    f) No, none of them

Please answer all of the following questions on a scale of 0 to 10, where 0 means "not at all" and 10 means "to a great extent". To what extent, if at all, did you feel:

44. pressured to agree with ideas or arguments of others?
45. that your contributions made it into the recommendations?

Respect for members' privacy

46. To what extent, if at all, do you feel your privacy (from undesired attention) was protected in this process? Please answer all of the following questions on a scale of 0 to 10, where 0 means "not at all" and 10 means "to a great extent".

47. Did you have a choice or not about your identity being revealed at the end of the process?
    a) Yes
    b) No

48. Have you been approached by someone and offered more information or invited to exchange privately?
    a) Yes
    b) No

49. If you were offered more information or invited to exchange privately, who approached you?
    a) Someone working for the media
    b) Someone working for a private company or agency
    c) Someone working for a non-governmental organisation
    d) Other (please specify)
    e) I don't know

50. Do you know if any other members of the group received approaches from media/interest groups?
    a) Yes, they did
    b) I suspect they did
    c) No, as far as I am aware
    d) I don't know

Annex D. Organiser questionnaire

The questions below are listed in the order of the criteria they are tailored to measure to facilitate their use for evaluation and interpretation. It is recommended that all questions are included as a minimum evaluation. They are intentionally non-leading and open-ended. Questions can be used as a survey, or to guide an interview. The answers should then be analysed with an interpretive approach, judging how answers provided compare with and are in coherence with results from the members' survey, document review and other measurement methods used for evaluation.

1) Process design integrity

Clear and suitable purpose

1. What were your objectives in organising this process?
2. What policy problem was the process addressing?
3. What was the mandate that the members of a deliberative process were given?
4. In your view, was organising a deliberative process in this situation a helpful way to address the policy issue? Why?

Clear and unbiased framing

5. In your view, how well did the members of the process receive and understand the question?

Suitable design

6. What are your overall impressions about the way the process went?
7. Did you achieve the objectives that were set out for this process?

Procedural design involvement

8. What was the process of setting the question, the mandate, and the design?
9. Were stakeholders relevant to the policy issue active in providing input?
10. Please list some of the stakeholder groups which were involved.
11. Who had a final say in the design questions of the deliberative process?

Transparency and governance

12. Did you use any terms of reference, rules of engagement, codes of conduct, or ethical frameworks that govern the process? (If yes, please provide them for reference.)
13. If yes, were they helpful?

Representativeness and inclusiveness

14. How did you recruit members of the process? Please describe the process.
15. Were there any groups that you found hard to reach? If yes, how did you address this challenge?

2) Deliberative experience

Neutrality and inclusivity of facilitation

16. What were the main tasks of facilitators?
17. How were the facilitators trained?
18. Were there any situations where some members were dominating the discussions? If yes, how did you manage this?

Accessible, neutral, and transparent use of online tools

[If online tools were used]

19. How did you choose the online tools to use?
20. Did you have to provide substantive explanations and assist with the use of online tools?
21. Would you use the same online tools for other deliberative processes in the future? If yes, why? If not, why not?

Breadth, diversity, clarity, and relevance of the evidence and stakeholders provided

22. What was the process of preparing the information base presented to members of the deliberative process? (Such as choosing relevant evidence and identifying stakeholders for presentations and panel discussions.)?

Quality of judgement

23. What deliberative techniques did you use? This could include considering underlying values, weighing of alternatives and trade-offs, exploring uncertainties, and considering different viewpoints.
24. What were some of the most conflicting viewpoints of the members? Please list them.

Perceived knowledge gains by participants

25. Did you notice any changes, over time, in the argumentation that members used to convey their point of view?

Accessibility and equality of opportunity to speak

26. Did you receive any feedback or suggestions from members to modify or adapt parts of the process?

Respect and mutual comprehension

27. Did you have to intervene to stop any conflicts amongst members?

28. Did you have to remind members to listen when others were speaking?
29. Did you feel like the group could listen to and incorporate challenging viewpoints from more marginalised members of society?

Free decision-making and response

30. Did you perceive any inappropriate external interference? For example, participants receiving undesired attention from lobbyists or media.
31. Could you describe the process of drafting the final recommendations?
32. In your view, were the democratic decision rules used for final decision making helpful in reaching an optimal decision? If yes, why? If not, why not?

Respect for participants' privacy

33. What was your approach to protecting members' privacy?

3) Pathways to impact

Member aftercare

34. What is your approach to fostering the community of members and the relationships they built throughout the deliberative process?

Annex E. Questions for organiser reflection

Organiser discussions for self-reflection can be open-ended. Some of the key questions that can help lead the discussion:

1. What went well and what did not go well at each stage of the process?
2. What surprised you or was unexpected?
3. What should we do differently next time? How could different parts of the process be improved next time?
4. How does the deliberative process measure against the OECD Good Practice Principles for Deliberative Processes for Public Decision Making? (Annex B)

Annex F. Table of comparison of existing frameworks of evaluating representative deliberative processes

Table F.1. Comparison of evaluation criteria of existing frameworks of evaluation for deliberative processes

Criteria of evaluation	Democracy in Motion: Evaluating the Practice and Impact of Deliberative Civic Engagement (2012)	OECD Good Practice Principles (2020)	Deliberative Processes in Practice (2016)	Deliberating Competence: Theoretical and Practitioner Perspectives on Effective Participatory Appraisal Practice (2008)	A Three-Stage Evaluation of a Deliberative Event on Climate Change and Transforming Energy (2008)	The Co-creation radar: a comprehensive public participation evaluation model (2019)	Involve (2021)	Jefferson Centre: Citizens Jury Handbook (2004)	Democracy Matters: Lessons from the 2015 Citizens' Assemblies on English Devolution (2016)	Evaluation of the Scottish Parliament's Citizens' Panels on Primary Care (2019)	Innovation in Democracy Programme Evaluation (2020)
Context evaluation (cultural/political contextual analysis in which deliberative civic engagement takes place)						Comparison					
						X					
1) Design integrity											
Unbiased framing	Transparent process by which issues are framed for deliberation	X	X	X		X					

Category	Criterion							
Procedural design involvement	Deliberative procedures developed in consultation with interested parties				X			
	Resulting process in line with best practices of deliberation (learning, deliberation, decision-making)	X		X	X	X		
	Equal opportunity to participate	X	X		X			
Representativeness	Final group - representative of general population	X		X	X	X	X	X
	Inclusivity: presence of permanent minorities & identity groups	X		X	X			
2) Democratic deliberation and judgements								
Deliberative analytic process (evaluation of the talk that takes place)	Create a solid information base		X	X	X		X	X
	Prioritize the key values at stake			X				
	Identify a broad range of solutions			X	X			
	Weighing Pros and Cons, trade-offs	X		X			X	
Democratic social process (evaluation of the social component of deliberation)	Equality of opportunity to speak/ adequately distributed speaking opportunities	X	X	X	X	X	X	X
	Ensuring mutual comprehension	X		X				
	Consideration of other ideas and experiences	X	X	X	X		X	X
	Respect of other participants			X	X		X	X
Sound judgement (evaluation of the quality of the final	Final decision making is uncoercive, uses one of any possible democratic voting systems and							

	decision or judgment)	decision rules (consensus, majority rule, proportional outcomes etc.)									
		Citizens' judgments become more enlightened as deliberation progresses		X				X	X		
		After deliberation participants demonstrate more informed and coherent views, provide reasoning and explain arguments underlying alternative points of view			X			X	X		
3) Influential conclusions and/or actions											
	Influential recommendations	When a clear majority of panellists favours a policy initiative, its chances of prevailing amongst policy makers should increase	X	X	X						X
	Effective, coordinated action (for those deliberative processes that attempt direct action)	Deliberative body is able to coordinate their post deliberative efforts		X	X						
4) Long-term effects on public life											
	Transforming public attitudes and habits	Stable or rising levels of public trust, signs of reduced civic neglect				X		X			
		Potential increase of voter turnout in elections									
		Increased sense of efficacy/political self-confidence				X		X	X		
		Developing more favourable views of the									

Changing public officials' attitudes/behaviour	judgments citizens make during deliberative events							
	Awareness of the importance of citizen deliberation						X	
	Changed attitudes toward the prospects of deliberation							
Altering strategic political choices	Initiative and policy campaigns focus more on addressing issues raised by deliberative panels							
	Routine pilot-testing of potential policy initiatives with deliberative processes							
Additional criteria	Process design and all other materials made public; response to recommendations and monitoring of their implementation; respect for participants' privacy; evaluation plan.	Publicity of outcomes and their rationales; existence of processes for appeal, review/iteration.	Efficiency - process is cost-effective and timely.	In addition: group ownership of the agenda of deliberative process; the process was documented thoroughly	Appropriate and accessible digital tools used; what type of evaluation was planned; balance of quality of implementation and resources used; effects on the organisation commissioning/organising participation;	Participant support for the use of deliberative process increased as a result.	Broader community engagement (opportunities for structured public engagement- public hearings, discussions etc). Truthfulness - participants were speaking what was truly on their mind. Unbiased facilitation - facilitations did not put forward their views.	Framing of the question - sufficiently challenging, carrying enough viable options to foster debate and deliberation. Transparency and communication about the purpose, activities and outcomes

	increased skills & capacities.		Influence of one or more participants over others - especially in deliberative processes where politicians take part. Process is fun.	to a wider public.

Source: OECD Good Practice Principles (2020), Deliberative Processes in Practice (2016), Deliberating Competence: Theoretical and Practitioner Perspectives on Effective Participatory Appraisal Practice (2008), A Three-Stage Evaluation of a Deliberative Event on Climate Change and Transforming Energy (2008), The Co-creation radar: a comprehensive public participation evaluation model (2019), The Co-creation radar: a comprehensive public participation evaluation model (2019), Involve participant survey (2021), Jefferson Centre: Citizens' Jury Handbook (2004), Democracy Matters: Lessons from the 2015 Citizens' Assemblies on English Devolution (2016), Evaluation of the Scottish Parliament's Citizens' Panels on Primary Care (2019), Innovation in Democracy Programme Evaluation (2020)

References

Brammall, S., Sisya, K., (2020). *Innovation in Democracy Programme Evaluation Report*, RENAISI

Caluwaerts, D. and Reuchamps, M., 2014. "Does Inter-Group Deliberation Foster Inter-Group Appreciation? Evidence from Two Experiments in Belgium." *Politics*, 34(2), pp.101-115, https://doi.org/10.1111/1467-9256.12043.

Chilvers, J. (2008). "Deliberating Competence: Theoretical and Practitioner Perspectives on Effective Participatory Appraisal Practice." *Science Technology Human Values* 33(2): 155-185.

Chwalisz, C. (2021), "The pandemic has pushed citizen panels online", *Nature* 589, 171, DOI: https://doi.org/10.1038/d41586-021-00046-7.

Edwards, Peter B.; Hindmarsh, Richard; Mercer, Holly; Bond, Meghan; and Rowland, Angela (2008) "A Three-Stage Evaluation of a Deliberative Event on Climate Change and Transforming Energy," *Journal of Public Deliberation*: Vol. 4: Iss. 1, Article 6.

Elstub, S., Carrick, J., and Khoban, Z. (2019) *Evaluation of the Scottish Parliament's Citizens' Panels on Primary Care*, Newcastle: Newcastle University.

Gastil, J., Broghammer, M., Rountree, J., & Burkhalter, S. (2019). "Assessment of Three 2018 Citizens' Initiative Review Pilot Projects." *University Park*, PA: Pennsylvania State University.

Healthy Democracy (2021). *Key Quality Elements of the Citizens' Initiative Review* [online] Available at: <https://healthydemocracy.org/cir/kqe/> [Accessed 26 May 2021].

Jefferson Centre (2004). *Citizens' Jury Handbook*.

Matthew Flinders, Katie Ghose, Will Jennings, Edward Molloy, Brenton Prosser, Alan Renwick, Graham Smith, Paolo Spada (2016). *Democracy Matters: Lessons from the 2015 Citizens' Assemblies on English Devolution*.

Nabatchi, T. (2012), A Manager's Guide to Evaluating Citizen Participation, IBM Center for The Business of Government

Nabatchi, Tina, John Gastil, Matt Leighninger, and G. Michael Weiksner (2012), *Democracy in Motion: Evaluating the Practice and Impact of Deliberative Civic Engagement*, Oxford: Oxford University Press, DOI:10.1093/acprof:oso/9780199899265.003.0010.

OECD (2021), *Eight Ways to Institutionalise Deliberative Democracy*, OECD Publishing, Paris.

OECD (2005), *Evaluating Public Participation in Policy Making*, OECD Publishing, Paris, https://doi.org/10.1787/9789264008960-en.

OECD (2020a), *Innovative Citizen Participation and New Democratic Institutions: Catching the Deliberative Wave*, OECD Publishing, Paris, https://doi.org/10.1787/339306da-en.

OECD (2020b), *Improving Governance with Policy Evaluation: Lessons From Country Experiences*, OECD Publishing, Paris, https://doi.org/10.1787/89b1577d-en.

Rask, M., Ertiö, T. (2019), *The Co-creation radar: a comprehensive public participation evaluation model*, University of Helsinki.

Rikki Dean, Felix Hoffmann, Brigitte Geissel, Stefan Jung and Bruno Wipfler, 2020, "Citizen Deliberation in Germany: Lessons from the 'Bürgerrat Demokratie'" Working Paper. Access at https://rikkidean.com/wp-content/uploads/2021/10/Citizen_Deliberation_Germany_WP_DEC20.pdf.

Smith, C., & Rowe, G. (2016). Deliberative Processes in Practice. In Dodds, S., & Ankeny, R. A. (Eds.). *Big Picture Bioethics: Developing Democratic Policy in Contested Domains*. Pages 59-70. Springer.

van der Does, R. and Jacquet, V., (2021). Small-Scale Deliberation and Mass Democracy: A Systematic Review of the Spillover Effects of Deliberative Minipublics. *Political Studies*, https://doi.org/10.1177/00323217211007278

www.ingramcontent.com/pod-product-compliance
Ingram Content Group UK Ltd.
Pitfield, Milton Keynes, MK11 3LW, UK
UKHW051300180426
11947UKWH00020B/1812